D1233843

Published by Creative Education
123 South Broad Street, Mankato, Minnesota 56001
Creative Education is an imprint of The Creative Company

Designed by Stephanie Blumenthal
Production Design by Melinda Belter

Photographs for Grant Heilman Photography, Inc., Christi Carter (25s), John Colwell (6s, 13), Linda Dufurrena
(14, 15), Grant Heilman (4s, 8, 9, 10, 11s, 20, 25, 31, 32), Thomas Hovland (16s), Lou Jacobs (20s), Larry
Lefever (cover, 4, 8s, 10s, 12, 13s, 14s, 16, 17, 22, 23, 24, 26, 27s, 30), Gary McMichael (18), Alan Pitcairn
(27), Runk/Schoenberger (6, 7s, 19s, 28s), Arthur C. Smith III (1, 19, 28), James Strawser (21s)

Library of Congress Cataloging-in-Publication Data

Richardson, Adele, 1966–
Farms / by Adele Richardson
p. cm. — (Let's Investigate)
Includes glossary
Summary: Examines the importance, structures, equipment,
operations, and different kinds of farms.
ISBN 0-88682-353-6
1. Agriculture—Juvenile literature. 2. Farms—Juvenile literature. [1. Farms. 2. Farm life. 3. Agriculture.]
I. Title. II. Series. III. Series: Let's Investigate (Mankato, Minn.)
S519.R48   1999
630—dc21   98-30294

First edition

2 4 6 8 9 7 5 3 1

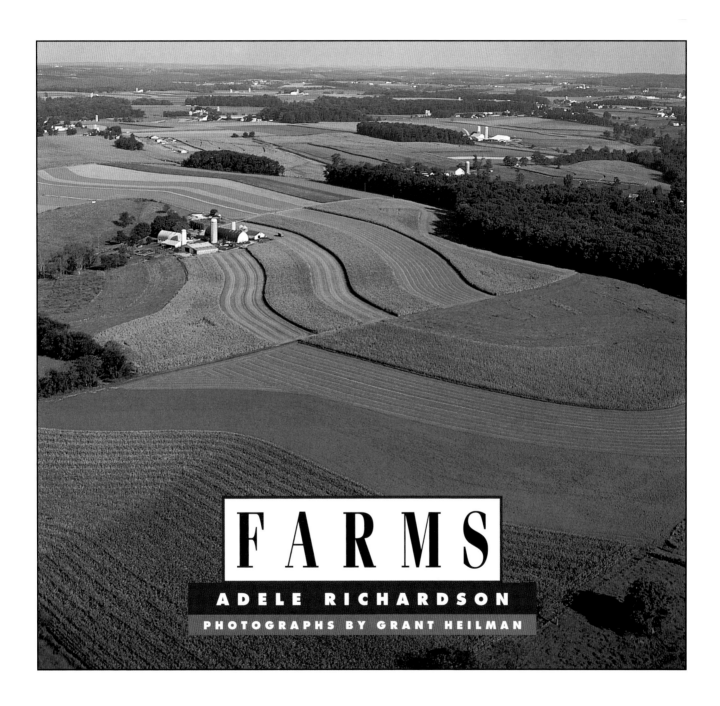

FARMS

ADELE RICHARDSON

PHOTOGRAPHS BY GRANT HEILMAN

Creative Education

FARM

arms are impor-tant to our lives. They provide us with the things we need, such as food, clothing, even furniture. There are many different kinds of farms, but one thing is common to all of them: hard work.

Corn is often grown and fed to animals on dairy farms

4

FARM
PICKERS

A mechanical cherry picker can do the work of 100 people all working at the same time.

*Above, barns are built in many shapes and sizes Right, an **Amish** barn-raising*

THE FIRST FARMS

Early humans were hunters and gatherers. They traveled in search of food, following herds of animals and seeking fruits and nuts. When the animals moved on, or an area ran out of food, the humans would leave to find more food.

Later, humans discovered they could grow a variety of foods in one place so they would not have to move around as much. Corn and wheat were among the foods that the first farmers grew on their farms.

P eople also dis-
covered that
certain animals
used for food could be
domesticated. It didn't
take long for the idea of
farming to spread all
around the world.

Discoveries of
ancient villages have
proven that farming has
existed for thousands of
years. It isn't known
exactly when, or where,
farming was first invent-
ed. It could have been in
Asia, South America, or
Africa.

FARM
HELPERS

*Instead of chemical
pesticides, ladybugs
are sometimes put
on plants to snack on
aphids, tiny insects
that damage crops.*

7

**Ladybugs help control
harmful pests**

FARM

In the 19th century, some American farmers living on the prairie built houses made from sod, big bricks of earth with the grass and roots still in place.

8

**Right, sunflowers just forming seeds
Center, workers knocking ripe cranberries off the plants**

oday, farming has become a business and is being influenced by science. Farmers use computers and technology to constantly improve farm production. Many people study **agribusiness** in college and then specialize in raising one type of plant or animal.

CROP FARMS

Farmers must choose a crop that will grow best in the **climate** where they live. Many North American farmers grow wheat, which requires a slightly drier and cooler climate. Countries with hot, wet climates often raise foods such as rice, cocoa, or tea. Bananas can even be grown in the jungle.

The method of "strip farming" conserves water and nutrients

MYTH

Tomatoes, squash, eggplants, okra, cucumbers, and pumpkins are vegetables.

TRUTH

All of these food items are really fruits!

Above, planting potatoes
Right, harvesting tea

More than half the farms in the United States are crop farms. To make enough money to live, farmers who grow field crops need large areas of land. Potatoes, cotton, pineapples, and peanuts are field crops. Corn, soybeans, wheat, barley, and rye are the most important types of field crops grown.

They are used to make everything from bread and breakfast cereal to margarine and snack chips. Even pet foods are made from corn, wheat, and rice.

Grains are grown for one of two reasons. A farmer may use the grain to feed livestock, or it may be sold for use in food products, for plastics manufacturing, even for ethanol, a fuel used to power cars and trucks. Farmers who sell grain for money operate what are called "cash grain" farms.

Some farmers grow various crops or raise livestock as well. The number of these "mixed farms" has fallen during the last 150 years. Today, only about five percent of U.S. farms are mixed farms.

FARM
F A C T

By the nineteenth century, 90 percent of the population of the United States owned or worked on a farm. By 1950 it was only 11 percent.

Ripe wheat

FARM
BALES

LIVESTOCK FARMS

Livestock farms provide us with **dairy** products, meat, eggs, and **poultry.** Chickens, turkeys, pigs, cattle, and sheep are some of the animals found on livestock farms. Many farmers keep just one kind of animal.

These turkeys are ready for market

Pigs, the first animals ever kept on farms, are the only mammals other than humans that can get sunburned.

13

Left, these steers weigh up to 2,000 pounds (907 kg)
Below, six-week-old feeder pigs at 30 pounds (13.6 kg)

Traditionally, livestock farms required as much, or more, land as field crop farms because animals were raised from birth through adulthood. Today, however, many farmers build feedlots, which take up very little space—perhaps 10 to 20 acres (24–48 hectares)—and function to produce meat for sale in large quantities.

FARM
ROBOTS

To scare off birds, some farmers use computer-programmed scare-crows that move electronically.

Above, young chicks at an automatic feeder Right, thoroughbred mare and foal

Animals in a feedlot live in buildings with a controlled environment. Air conditioners and heaters keep the temperature constant, and the animals are fed a special diet that makes them grow quickly. One feedlot might contain only females that give birth and nurse their offspring for a few weeks, another feedlot might take the young animals and house them for three months or so, and still another feedlot might contain only adult animals that will soon be sold.

15

Beef cattle

Ranches are open farms where beef cattle are raised. Most livestock farms in the western half of the United States are ranches because there are large areas of grasslands that cattle can eat.

Farmers raise cattle for milk on dairy farms. The milk is sold to drink and is also used to make cheese and butter. A refrigerated tanker truck transports milk from a dairy farm to a **creamery,** sometimes twice a day.

FARM
FACT

The average size of a farm in 1940 was 174 acres (70.5 hectares). By 1974 that number had risen to 385 acres (156 hectares).

Above, geese and ducks
Right, dairy cow
Opposite, round hay bales dot the landscape

Chickens, turkeys, and ducks are raised for meat also, and many farms exist for the production of chicken eggs. Sheep and goats provide not only meat and milk, but their fur, called wool, is often used to make clothing. Rabbits are also raised both for food and for their fur.

Horses are not raised for food, but they are sometimes kept on farms as pets or working animals. Some ranches raise only horses that will become race horses —often worth thousands or even million of dollars.

FARM

18

FARM

TECHNOLOGY

Some cows wear necklaces that send messages to a computer. The computer records when the cow ate and when it was last milked.

Harvested catfish

A VARIETY OF FARMS

Not all livestock are domesticated. Bees, for example, are raised in man-made beehives, and the honey they produce is collected and sold at market. Some livestock are raised for their fur. These include minks and chinchillas. Fish farmers raise fish and shellfish to sell for food. Often, they use methods that help the fish grow bigger and faster than they would in the wild.

FARM
FICTION

Long ago, farmers believed that if a pig carried straw in its mouth, a storm was coming, and if sheep fed on a hill, good weather was ahead.

19

The fish live inside cages in ponds, lakes, rivers, even oceans. Sometimes the animals are put in large tanks that are built on land. Fish farms, like other farms, are located in a climate that best suits their needs. Salmon and trout need fresh water and live best in cooler temperatures. Shellfish, such as lobsters, live in saltwater and grow better in warmer temperatures.

*Left, harvested crayfish
Above, honey bee*

FARM
HOUSES

20

Above, 10-week-old pine trees
Right, plum orchard

Nurseries are farms that grow plants and flowers. Many florists get their flowers from nurseries. Various herbal medicines, such as ginseng and garlic, are grown for sale to health food companies.

Most nurseries are located in greenhouses, or hothouses, made of plastic or glass. By letting in sunlight while keeping out the cold, a greenhouse allows plants to grow all year long. Water is usually sprayed on the plants from pipes near the ceiling of the greenhouse.

Some farmers raise trees that bear nuts, such as walnuts or cashews, and fruit, such as oranges or apples. These are called orchards. Not all tree farms produce fruit, however. Sugar maple trees produce maple syrup, and many kinds of trees are raised for lumber. Christmas tree farms provide many people with a special product just once a year!

FARM FAMILIES

The are millions of "subsistence farms" in the world. Each of these farms grows only enough food to feed the family that lives and works on it.

Stanley plums

FARM

EGGS

Egg farms can have hundreds, even thousands, of hens. Once the eggs are laid, they gently drop to conveyor belts that remove them from the henhouse.

*Above, chicken house
Right, dairy farm*

THE FARMSTEAD

Depending on the type of products raised, a variety of different buildings make up a farmstead. Except for some feedlot owners, most farmers live on their land, so a farmhouse is sure to be a part of the farmstead. Farmers who grow grains store them in a **granary** until they are ready to be sold, and some farmers put ears of corn into **corn cribs.**

Most farmers also have a barn in which they store straw and hay. If horses and cows are kept in the barn too, the hay is stacked in the **hayloft** to prevent the animals from eating it.

Corn and a type of grass called alfalfa are often fed to livestock in the winter. This **silage** is stored in tall, airtight structures called **silos.**

FARM
FURRY

A sheep's tail hangs down; a goat's tail stands up. A male "billy" goat has chin fur that looks like a beard; a male "ram" sheep has no beard.

23

FARM
NICKNAME

The large blades on a plow that cut into the earth are called plowshares. They are strong enough to dig up large rocks.

FARM
CRAWLER

A tractor with steel tracks instead of rubber tires is called a crawler. They are used for moving over rocky ground.

FARM
LEADERS

Russia and the U.S. are the top two wheat growing countries in the world, feeding millions of people all around the globe.

Harvested tobacco hangs to dry in the sun

Dairy farms have a milk house, or milk shed. The cows are brought into this building twice a day and connected to milking machines. Chicken farms will have a brooder house, where newly hatched chicks are kept, and a hen house, where the females lay eggs.

Other farms have sheds to store freshly picked fruits and vegetables. Farm machinery is kept in storage sheds or barns. From cattle or horse barns and hen houses to milking parlors and calf stalls, every farmstead building has a purpose. It's easy to tell what a farmer grows or raises just by looking at the various buildings on the farmstead.

25

Left, corn is put into a storage elevator
Above, walnut orchard

*There are more
sheep and goats on
farms all over the
world than any other
domestic animal.*

26

FARM MACHINERY

Machines, often large, heavy ones, are an important part of farm work. Many crop farms have at least one tractor that pulls a plow. The plow tills the soil, digging it up and turning it over. Tilling makes it easier to plant seeds. If the soil needs to be more finely crushed, a farmer pulls a "harrow" over the earth. Set with either spikes, disks, or teeth, the harrow crushes the earth into a smooth planting surface.

Planting tobacco

27

Left, baling Bermuda grass
Above, laying sod, or healthy grass

At planting time, a seed drill, also called a grain drill, makes holes in the soil and drops in the seeds. Some crops, such as potatoes and cotton, need lots of water. An **irrigation** system may be used to water dry crops.

Harvesting must be done quickly to prevent spoilage. On today's farms, machines do most of the hard work. A combine harvester is used for wheat, soybeans, and corn. The machine cuts and separates the grain from the stalks automatically, collecting the grain in a storage bin and tossing the stalks back out into the field to be left as **mulch.**

FARM
SOIL

Some crops, such as wheat, grow best in soil containing a lot of humus, which is decayed plants or small animals.

Below, the pink bollworm is a threat to crops Right, often teams of combine harvesters work in large fields

Cotton-pickers remove cotton from the plants. Machines called balers pick up hay or straw and either press or roll it into bundles called bales. Some machines even automatically feed animals and give them medicine. Machines now exist to help the farmer with almost every job on the farm.

Someday tractors may need no drivers. These machines would be controlled by computers and guided by radar.

FARM
CLONES

*Potatoes are actually clones of other potatoes because they can reproduce without **pollination** by another plant.*

29

Science is helping today's farmers produce bigger and better crops and livestock. Chemicals have been developed that enrich the soil and control weeds and pests that may harm crops. But too many chemicals can damage the earth and poison water.

Organic farming cuts down on the risks of chemical pollution because organic farms don't use chemicals or pesticides. Instead, they rely on natural materials to fertilize soil and control weeds and insects.

FARM

A grease band is something farmers tie around the trunks of fruit trees to keep damaging insects from crawling up.

Above, scarecrows can be fun as well as useful Right, computerized milking parlors are efficient Opposite, irrigating crops in a dry area

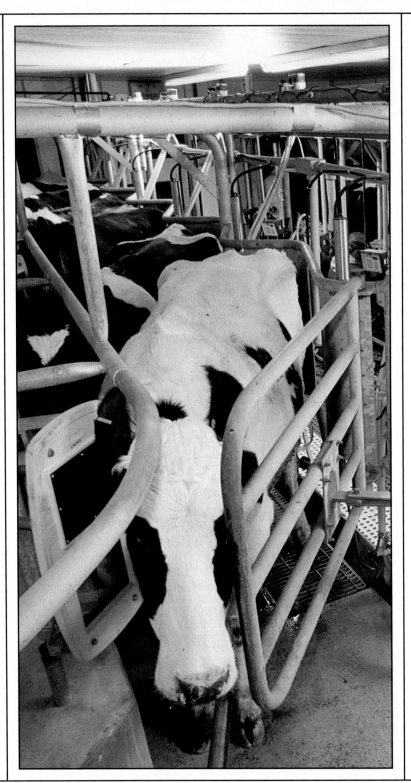

Hydroponics is another method of farming. Plants are grown in large tanks of water without soil. The water is enriched with **nutrients** that would normally come from soil. The tanks can be housed indoors to keep pests and bad weather from damaging the crops. Astronauts have even experimented with hydroponics on board the space shuttle!

From hydroponics to computer-operated farm machinery, from chemical advances to **genetics** research, farming is constantly advancing. These are just a few steps in the development of a science that will take the business of farming into the future.

Glossary

Agribusiness is the industry of farming, from the production and sale of farm machinery, to farming operations, to the making, storing, and selling of farm products such as grain and livestock.

The **Amish** are a group of people who live simple lives and have a strong religious faith and sense of community.

An area's **climate** is the average type of weather determined over several years.

Corn cribs are large rectangular or round bins made of wooden timbers covered with wire mesh.

A creamery is a factory where milk and cheese products are made and sold.

Dairy products include milk and foods that are made from milk, such as cheese, butter, and yogurt.

Domesticated animals have been tamed enough to be around humans.

Genetics is a branch of biology that deals with how plant and animal characteristics are passed on from organisms to their offspring .

Seeds or grain that has been separated from its stalks is sometimes stored in a **granary.**

A **hayloft,** sometimes also called a haymow, is the area of a building where hay is stored to keep it clean and dry.

Methods of **irrigation,** such as the laying of pipes or digging of streams and ditches, provide dry land with water.

Mulch is a covering of broken plant stalks, straw, or leaves that is left on the earth to prevent moisture loss and weed growth.

Nutrients are chemical substances that promote growth and health in the living things that consume them.

Anything **organic** is free from chemicals or additives.

Pollination is the transfer of pollen from one plant to another; pollination is needed for plants to reproduce.

Domesticated birds, such as chickens, ducks, turkeys, or geese, that are raised for meat or eggs are called **poultry.**

A **silo** is a tall round structure, usually built next to a barn, in which **silage** is stored; silage is food for livestock made from grasses and grains.

Topsoil is the upper layer of soil that farmers turn over when they plow; this layer is where plants have most of their roots.

Index